Piano In Color

Parent Guide

2013 Edition

Julia Tulloch

ISBN: **1478200782**
ISBN-13: **978-1478200789**

Welcome to Piano In Color, and congratulations on becoming your preschooler's first piano teacher. This guide is to be read alongside the *Piano In Color: Music Lessons for Mini-Musicians* book.

Specially written for parents who do not have a musical background, this easy to read manual contains the guidelines you need to teach your mini-musician to play the songs in the *Piano In Color: Music Lessons for Mini-Musicians* book. Don't be surprised if you find that you too, are learning to play the piano!

The following symbols are used in this guide.

- This indicates a section to be read to your preschooler. Feel free to tailor the vocabulary to your mini-musician's understanding.

- This indicates instructions/guidelines for the parent.

You and your preschooler will find it helpful to listen to each song before learning to play it. Visit www.pianoInColor.com/extras, where you will find free recordings of all the songs and other freebies.

Have fun learning and playing!

Julia Tulloch

Contents

Getting Started

1. Adding Colors

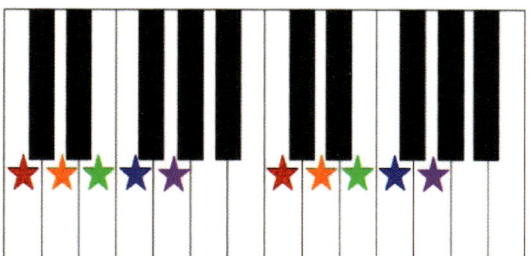

 First of all, you will need to add the colors to the piano as indicated on pages four and five of ***Piano In Color: Music Lessons for Mini-Musicians.*** The colors are on the keys named C, D, E, F and G, but your preschooler will learn them as **Red Note**, **Orange Note**, **Green Note**, **Blue Note** and **Purple Note**.

2. Finger Numbers

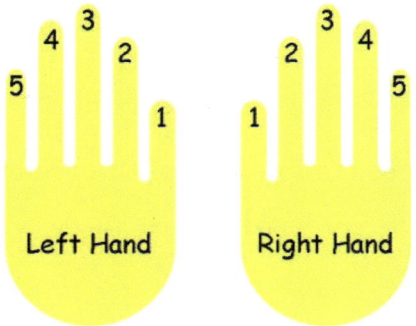

There is one finger for each colored sticker. Note that on both hands, the thumb is finger 1 and the little finger is finger 5.

3. Introducing Notes

Your mini-musician is going to learn to play five notes with each hand. Each note has a finger number on it and matches the color of one of the colored stickers. For example:

 This means use finger 1 of the right hand (thumb) to play the "red" piano key – i.e. the key with the red sticker on it.

 This means use finger 2 of the right hand (index finger) to play the "orange" piano key.

 The left hand notes have their stems (lines) going downwards instead of upwards. This means use finger 5 of the left hand to play the "red" piano key.

 This symbol is called a rest, but we are going to call it "Freeze" (as in the "freeze dance" game). This means "stop playing and pause for a second."

Imagine a clock ticking while your preschooler is playing: "tick, tick, tick, tick." Your child should play a note (or say "Freeze" if there is a **Freeze Sign**) on each tick of the clock. You can set the initial speed of this imaginary clock as slow or as fast as she is comfortable with, but once the song starts, the speed should not change.

At first her speed will vary as she is working out which keys to play, but once she is comfortable with the notes in the lesson you are working on, help her to maintain a consistent pace. Saying "tick, tick, tick, tick" evenly, while she is playing, will remind her not to speed up or slow down.

4. Sitting at the Piano.

Have your preschooler sit up straight at the center of the piano. The stickers on the right are around the center point. He should sit in front of these stickers to be at the right place. Make sure he can easily reach the piano keys. He may need to use a cushion if the piano stool is not adjustable. If his feet don't reach the floor, rest them on a small stool so they are not swinging back and forth.

5. Lessons and Practice

Read through each lesson before you work through it with your child. The lessons are very brief and will take only 2 or 3 minutes for you to read and understand. Don't overwhelm your mini-musician by covering too many lessons too quickly. One lesson per week is adequate.

Once you have introduced a lesson to your child, then use the rest of the week for practicing what was learned in the lesson. Even if your preschooler instantly grasps the lesson and plays it perfectly first time, the practice is still essential.

Practice time should be short and fun. Ideally, practice time should last 5 to 10 minutes each day. Sit with your child during practice time – preschoolers are generally too young to practice alone. During practice time, your mini-musician should play each song from the lesson at least twice. If there are any parts of a song that she finds difficult, have her repeat those sections three or four times before trying the whole song again. End practice time by playing one or two songs that were learned in previous lessons to ensure that she doesn't forget what she has already learned.

Some songs will be learned quickly while others will take a little longer. Don't move on to the next lesson until she has mastered the current one. Remember to offer lots of praise and encouragement after each lesson. A round of applause after each good performance helps too!

So now you are ready to start teaching your preschooler Piano In Color. At the beginning of each practice time, remind him to:

- sit correctly at the piano;
- put one finger over each "colored" piano key;
- curve his fingers slightly as if he is holding a ball.

At the end of each practice time, remember to update the practice chart at the back of this book.

Now he is ready to begin!

Right Hand Notes

We are going to begin by learning five notes for the Right Hand. The notes are introduced one at a time.

You may need to point to each note as your mini-musician plays it. There are a lot of notes, and it is easy for young children to lose sight of which note to play. Point to the **Freeze Signs** too, and make sure she says "freeze" for each one.

Lesson 1 – Red Note

 The first note we are going to learn is **Red Note** for the right hand.

Whenever we see this **Red Note**, we are going to play it (press it down) with finger 1 (thumb) and say "Red" or "One". Each time we play it, we can say "Red" because it is **Red Note**, or we can say "One" because we play it with finger 1.

Whenever we see a **Freeze Sign**, we are not going to play any notes – we're just going to say "Freeze".

 Parent, if possible, begin this lesson by listening to the recording of the Red Note song. Follow the music notes on the page with your finger while listening to show your child how the notes on the page and the music on the piano work together.

When your mini-musician is ready to try playing it, encourage her **not** to look at the piano keys while she is playing, but to follow the notes on the page as you point to them instead.

Lesson 2 – Orange Note

 The second note we are going to learn is **Orange Note** for the right hand.

We are going to play **Orange Note** with finger 2 (index finger) of our right hand and say "Orange" or "Two" while we play it. Saying the numbers while we play helps our fingers to remember where the piano keys are.

It is important for your mini-musician to say "freeze" at the **Freeze Signs**. There are a lot of them in this tune. The **Freeze Signs** are just as important as the notes, and saying "freeze" will help your mini-musician to not miss them.

The note numbers indicate the number of the finger that plays that note, so saying the note numbers is more important than saying the note colors. If your preschooler prefers to say the colors, have him play the song an extra time so he has a chance to say the numbers too.

Lesson 3 – Freeze Tag

Let's try playing two different notes in the same song. "Freeze Tag" uses the two notes we have learned so far. Remember to play **Red Note** with finger 1 and **Orange Note** with finger 2, and don't forget to say the note numbers while you play the keys.

After the first few attempts, emphasize the importance of looking at the notes on the page while playing, and not at the piano keys. It may help to hold a sheet of paper above your mini-musician's fingers while she plays so that she can't see her hands even if she is tempted to look down at them.

It can take a few lessons for your preschooler to believe that she can find the keys without looking at her fingers, but she can!

Lesson 4 – Green Note

Our next right hand note is **Green Note** which we are going to play with finger 3 (middle finger).

In this tune, we also have 3 **Freeze Signs** next to each other. When we see them, we are not going to play any notes – we are just going to say "freeze, freeze, freeze".

There is often a temptation to say "freeze, freeze, freeze" very quickly. Remind your preschooler of the ticking clock and that there should be one "freeze" on each tick of the clock. Easy parts of the music should not be played any faster than the more difficult parts. Everything should be the same speed as our ticking clock.

Lesson 5 – Follow Me

There is a lot to think about in this song with three different colored notes and the freezes, but you can do it!

Be careful on the second line. There are no freezes until the very end of this line, so try to play without stopping until you reach the freeze.

As before, after the first couple of attempts, emphasize the importance of looking at the notes on the page and not at the piano keys while playing.

Remember that the songs are available free online for you and you mini-musician to listen to at www.pianoInColor.com/extras. Hearing the recorded performances will give him a good idea of what he is aiming for.

Lesson 6 – Itsy Bitsy Spider

Here is a song that you may know. It includes everything we have learned so far. There isn't a nice pattern to the notes like we had with the previous songs, but the good thing about it is that you probably know the song, and once you have learned to play it, you can sing the words while you play!

Let your mini-musician focus on saying note numbers and freezes before trying to sing the words. It will take quite a bit of practice for him to play this without looking at his fingers, so revisit some of the previously learned tunes so he doesn't get tired of working on "Itsy Bitsy Spider".

Lesson 7 – Blue Note

Finger 4 plays **Blue Note.** Finger 4 is not an easy finger to control. You may find that finger 3 wants to play too whenever you try to play a note with finger 4, so you will have to really concentrate while practicing this tune!

Remind your mini-musician to keep her fingers close to the piano keys while playing this tune. At first, she may raise the other fingers up high in an attempt to control finger 4 and to play the **Blue Note**. The goal is to be able to play this tune without the other fingers flying up high.

Lesson 8 – Upside Down / Almost Yankee Doodle

Now let's try a couple of tunes with all the colors we've learned so far. "Upside Down" has lots of **Blue Notes** in it, so this will give you good practice at controlling finger 4. "Almost Yankee Doodle" has only one **Blue Note**, so you might find it a little easier than "Upside Down."

There are two songs in this lesson, so you may need to extend the daily practice time by a few minutes.

Lesson 9 – Purple Note / Rainbow

Our last right hand note is **Purple Note**. We are going to play this note with finger 5. Finger 5 is not as strong as the other fingers, but with practice it will play just as well as the other fingers.

Once you can play Purple Note, we will try "Rainbow" which uses all five colors.

Lesson 10 – Mary Had A Little Lamb

Here is another familiar song. While learning this song, we are also going to learn some dynamics. **Dynamics** is the word used to describe how loudly or softly we play our music. Our first dynamic is "*piano*" (*p*), which is the Italian word for "soft". When you see a *p* in your music, it means you must play quietly by pressing the keys gently.

The term "dynamics" is used to describe many other aspects of playing music, but in this book, volume is the only dynamic we will be learning.

A touch-sensitive keyboard sounds louder when you press hard on the keys and sounds softer when you press the keys lightly. If you have a touch-sensitive keyboard, then after your mini-musician has learned this tune, you can introduce the idea of playing softly and she can try it out.

Not all keyboards are touch-sensitive. If your keyboard is not touch-sensitive then she will not be able to include these dynamics in her playing. It is still a good idea to explain what *p* means and perhaps just turn the keyboard volume down while she plays this song so she remembers the meaning of *p*.

Lesson 11 – Jingle Bells

Jingle Bells is a cheerful Christmas song, so this time, our dynamic is "*forte*" (*f*), which is the Italian word for "loud". When you see an *f* in your music, press the piano keys harder to make them sound louder. Once you've mastered it, feel free to sing along while you play.

The last five notes of this song are the trickiest. Your mini-musician may be tempted to play a green note between the blue and the orange note. If he keeps slipping up on this, then draw a box around these five notes and have him practice these boxed notes three or four times before playing through the whole song.

Again, if your keyboard is not touch-sensitive, create the dynamic by turning the volume a little higher. This way your mini-musician will remember the meaning of *f*.

Left Hand Notes

Parent, you have done a great job getting your mini-musician through all the right hand notes.

Remember to visit the right hand songs from time to time while learning the left hand notes. From now on, it is a good idea to begin practice time with one of the latter right hand songs (**Rainbow**, **Mary Had A Little Lamb** or **Jingle Bells**). This will help her to retain all her right hand skills while learning the left hand notes

Have your mini musician say the note numbers while playing these left hand songs. Now that she has grasped the basic idea of the color notes, the focus is solely on the numbers rather than the colors.

Lesson 12 – Red Note / Orange Note / Duet

Let's begin with **Red Note** and **Orange Note** for the left hand.

Notice that the stems (lines) on the left hand notes go downwards instead of upwards. Another thing to notice is that the left hand's **Red Note** has a number 5 on it. (Remember that right hand's **Red Note** had a number 1 on it). So with the left hand, **Red Note** is played with finger 5 (not with finger 1 as it is for the right hand).

Orange Note is a little tricky because it is played with finger 4. You may remember from earlier that finger 4 is not an easy finger to control, so this will take a little extra practice.

Lesson 13 – Green Note / The Slide

Green Note is the next left hand note we are going to learn. We play **Green Note** with finger 3.

We are also going to learn the **Repeat Sign**. The **Repeat Sign** means you must play the song twice. Both these songs have a **Repeat Sign** so don't forget to play them through twice.

Lesson 14 – Blue Note / Purple Note / Blast Off

The last two left hand notes are **Blue Note** and **Purple Note**. Fingers 1 and 2 are strong, easy to control fingers so you should have no problem with these. "Blast Off" uses all the five colors. Don't forget the freezes!

Lesson 15 – Row The Boat

This is our last left hand song. Once you have learned it, sing along while you play!

Two Hands Together.

These songs take a little more effort, but with practice, your preschooler will be sounding like a true mini-musician in no time at all!

He will often be playing two notes at the same time, so there is no need to say the note numbers any more. By now, he should know where all the keys are without looking at his fingers. Work through these songs thoroughly and make sure he can play each song well before starting on the next.

Lesson 16 – Reddy Orange

Let's begin playing with both hands at the same time. When you see a right hand note above a left hand note, then you must play both notes at the same time.

Parent, have your preschooler play **Red Note** with both hands together a few times before starting this song. It can take a little time for him to get his coordination together. The two notes should sound simultaneously, not sequentially.

Have him play very slowly through this tune, concentrating on sounding the notes simultaneously and remembering to say the "freezes."

Lesson 17 – Mary Had A Little Lamb

 You have played this song before with the right hand. Now you are going to play it with two hands together. First of all, play through the right hand part (remember that right hand notes are the ones with the stems going up).

Now, let's look at the left hand notes. The left hand plays the same color note all the way through this song. What color is it? Yes, that's right. Left hand *only* plays **Purple Note**. Even though it is quite easy, play through the left hand part.

Now let's try playing the first right hand note and the first left hand note at the same time. That's the right hand **Green Note** with the left hand **Purple Note**. Play them together, at the same time. That's a great sound! Try it a few times until it feels easy to do.

Good work! After playing **Green Note**, right hand then plays **Orange Note**, **Red Note** and then **Orange Note** again. Left hand plays nothing while right hand plays these three notes.

So after you play the first note of the song with both hands (right hand **Green Note** with the left hand **Purple Note**), then play the next three notes with right hand alone. Does that sound like the beginning of "Mary Had A Little Lamb"? Great, let's keep going.

 Next, both hands are going to play at the same time again. Right hand is going to play three **Green Notes**, while left hand plays three **Purple Notes**. Make sure that the green and purple notes sound at exactly the same time. Don't forget the Freeze afterwards.

Good work. Continue through the rest of the song.

Parent, this will be quite challenging at first, but stick with it. Once he has completed this song, playing with two hands begins to fall into place, and the music he plays is very rewarding.

If he is struggling with any part of the song, draw a box around the difficult part and have him repeat those boxed notes a few times until he can play that part with ease. It may help to remind him that left hand only plays **Purple Note**, so he doesn't have to think about playing any other left hand notes in this song.

Lesson 18 – Largo

 Largo is a famous piece of music, written by a composer named **Dvorak**.

Let's play through the right hand part first. Playing one hand at a time is called "playing hands separately".

This time, left hand has more than just **Purple Note** to play, so again, let's spend a little time playing through the left hand part too before trying to play it with two hands together.

 The last few notes on the first line of this song will probably need some isolated practice.

This is the first time that the left hand plays without the right hand in a Two Hands Together song, and it may take several attempts for your mini-musician to coordinate these notes correctly.

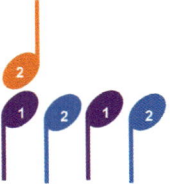

Lesson 19 – Ode to Joy

Ode to Joy was written by the famous composer, Beethoven. This is the longest song we have seen so far, so it will take a little longer to learn it. The left hand has only two notes – **Red Note** and **Purple Note**, so you will find that Ode to Joy is easier to play than it looks.

Rather than trying to play through the whole song, have your mini musician take it a line at a time. Once he can play one line comfortably with both hands, then he can start working on the next line. There is a lot of repetition in all the two page songs, so once he has learned the first page, he will find the second page quite easy to play.

These longer songs can each take a couple of weeks to master, so take your time working through them. Remember that letting your mini-musician hear the recordings before he starts to learn the songs, will make it easier for him to learn them.

Lesson 20 – Jingle Bells

You learned Jingle Bells for the right hand a while back, so this will feel familiar to you. Again, the left hand has only two notes – **Red Note** and **Purple Note**.

Jingle Bells starts with the same two notes as Ode to Joy, so let's start by playing the first right hand note and the first left hand note at the same time. That's the right hand **Green Note** with the left hand **Red Note** – play them together, at the same time.

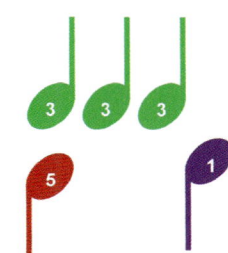

Great! Next the left hand stops playing while the right hand plays **Green Note**, **Green Note**. Finally, the left hand plays **Purple Note** while the right hand stops playing.

Great job! That sounds just like Jingle Bells!

Have your mini-musician practice the section above until he is playing it with ease, before continuing through the rest of the song line by line.

Lesson 21 – Lullaby For Lili

This song is for two hands, but you can see that there are no right hand notes on top of left hand notes. This means that there are no notes to be played at the same time. Pay attention to the stems to remind you which hand is to play each note. Remember that stems go up for right hand notes, and stems go down for left hand notes.

It may help to point to the tip of the stems of the notes as your mini-musician plays through this the first few times. Pointing "higher up" for right hand notes and "lower down" for left hand notes will help her to remember which hand to play with.

Lesson 22 – Irish Jig

This is our final two page song. In this song, the left hand has more colors than in the other songs you have learned.

This is the most challenging song in the book, so prepare to spend a little longer on it. As stated before, if any part proves difficult, draw a box around that section and have your preschooler repeat it several times until she is playing the boxed section with ease.

Alphabet Rollercoaster

The piano keys that your preschooler has learned as **Red Note**, **Orange Note**, **Green Note**, **Blue Note** and **Purple Note** are really called C, D, E, F and G. Have your mini-musician say the letter names while playing Alphabet Rollercoaster to help him learn the true note names.

Once your mini-musician has completed the ***Piano In Color: Music Lessons for Mini-Musicians*** book, he will be ready to start learning to play from Black-and-White notes (i.e. the musical staff). Contact a local piano teacher to get started.

Congratulations!

Piano In Color Practice Chart.

The following pages contain the Piano In Color Practice Chart. Each day that your mini-musician practices a song, check one of the boxes next to that song. The song must be played at least twice to merit a check for that day.

After 5 days of practice, she should be ready for the next song. If she hasn't quite completed the song, spend a few more days on it before advancing to the next song.

When your mini-musician can play the song well without looking at the piano keys too much, put a check in the ⭐ box.

RIGHT HAND

Songs	Practice Check Off					⭐
Red Note						
Orange Note						
Freeze Tag						
Green Note						
Follow Me						
Itsy Bitsy Spider						
Blue Note						
Upside Down						
Almost Yankee Doodle						
Purple Note						
Rainbow						
Mary Had A Little Lamb						
Jingle Bells						

LEFT HAND

Songs	Practice Check Off					
Red Note						
Orange Note						
Duet						
Green Note						
The Slide						
Blue Note						
Purple Note						
Blast Off						
Row The Boat						

TWO HANDS TOGETHER

Songs	Practice Check Off				⭐
Reddy-Orange					
Mary Had A Little Lamb					
Largo					
Ode To Joy					
Jingle Bells					
Lullaby For Lili					
Irish Jig					
Alphabet Rollercoaster					

Printed in Great Britain
by Amazon.co.uk, Ltd.,
Marston Gate.